THE REAL GIRLS' GUIDE TO

Taking It All Off

A SMALL GROUP GUIDE FOR REMOVING THE LAYERS
BETWEEN YOU AND TRUE FRIENDSHIPS

Stephanie May Wilson

Stephanie *May* Wilson

©2015 Stephanie May Wilson
StephanieMayWilson.com

Published by For Every Story
foreverystory.com

FOR THE WOMEN WHO TAUGHT ME EVERYTHING I KNOW

ABOUT FRIENDSHIP & ABOUT LIFE

LAYERS

Throughout our lives, we accumulate layers. We put them on like clothes, piling them on top of one another until we're waddling through life fully covered. We put on the uniform of our job or our after school activities, we carefully select an outfit that will help us fit in, or stand out (in the best way of course). We put on our mom shoes, or the hat that deems us the "funny girl." We put on the glasses that make us look smart, and the makeup that hides our imperfections. We keep our house perfectly decorated, our profile photos perfectly selected, and our Instagrams perfectly filtered. We learn what's acceptable, what's reject-able, and we adjust accordingly. We build the walls that keep us from being exposed, or hurt, or worst of all, abandoned.

Our life is a journey of piling things onto ourselves—covering ourselves with layers and layers of how we want to be seen, and who others expect us to be. The more layers we pile on the harder it is for anyone to get to know us, for us to be able to show anyone who we truly are, for us ever to feel connected. Because to feel connected, to feel truly understood and loved, we have to be known—not for our layers but for the beating heart underneath them all.

So that's what we're doing. In the next 6 weeks, we're taking off the layers one by one. We're going to do the hard, beautiful work of revealing the true us to the women around our table, and the relationships that will form along the way will change our lives. Friendships like that always do.

WELCOME

To Be fully Seen by Somebody, then, & be Loved anyhow—this is a Human offering that can Border on Miraculous.

Elizabeth Gilbert

READ THIS OUT LOUD AT THE BEGINNING OF YOUR FIRST GATHERING

Hello and welcome! This is the very closest thing to having you all around my kitchen table, and I couldn't be more excited.

That's where I wish we were whenever I'm writing. In fact, it's what I picture as I'm sitting at my desk, or on the couch (more likely), typing strings of black words on the white page, and trying to feel cozy.

Because to me, the words aren't the point, the connection is. And my blog, my book, and this guide are the closest I can get to fitting us all around the table— stories and whoops of laughter filling my home like the smell of freshly baked cookies still warm from the oven.

So come in, and make yourself comfortable. I'm so glad you're here.

The journey we're embarking on is a great one, and I can't wait to get started.

THE PROBLEM

Have you ever scrolled through Instagram photos of dinner parties, and vacations, and gatherings wondering if you're the only person in the world who feels like an outsider?

Have you ever gazed longingly at a table of laughing women, wishing there was a seat reserved just for you?

Have you ever felt like you missed the boat on deep friendships, like it should have somehow happened already and now it might be too late?

I have.

Sometimes it's a set of circumstances that leaves us with loneliness rattling around in our bones. We move away, or our best friends move away, or our husband's job keeps us in a perpetual state of motion.

Sometimes we find ourselves in new season of life feeling like a freshman all over again—like we're starting from scratch and have no one to sit with at lunch.

Some of our stories include lots of moves and transition—we've never been in a place long enough to form those deep, soul-filling connections.

But sometimes we do have friends, lots of them in fact. But even that doesn't seem to quell the loneliness the way we wish it would. We have people to talk to at parties, and co-workers to invite over for dinner, but those friendships seem to be lacking something. We feel surrounded but not deeply so. Known, but not in the way that makes us feel like we're not alone.

No matter your story or how you got to this place, so many of us are walking around this earth feeling lonely. So many women feel disconnected, or left out, or like they'll never have the kind of connection their hearts so deeply crave.

There's an epidemic of loneliness in our world today, and I truly believe it's because of our layers. We talk to each other, but we don't really talk to each other. We rarely say the thing we need to say, the thing we need someone to know about us, the truth that would really set us free.

We keep our makeup perfect, and our dirty laundry hidden. We only let people see us when we have the world at our feet, when we're spinning the plates of our homes, and our families, and our jobs, and our perfectly-styled appearance all effortlessly, not even breaking a sweat.

But those outer things—our success and our perfectly blown out hair—aren't the real us. They may be the parts we want people to see, the protection we keep around our tender, beating hearts, but they're not the parts we need people to see.

When we're only known and loved at our best, we're left wondering if anyone will ever love us at our worst. Worst of all, we're left to face the world alone. Our layers and the illusion of perfection makes the world a lonely place.

So that's what we're here to fix. We're here to connect, to create and cultivate the kind of friendship that changes everything. And it starts with breaking right through the idea that we need to be perfect in order to be loved.

So today, right here, around this table, we are doing something audacious and truly, wonderfully terrifying. We're going to strip off that perfect façade and we're going to do it together.

I am on a mission, for you, for me, and for women everywhere to help us stop trying to be perfect, and start being us.

I am on a mission to give all of us the courage to be who we were meant to be—to bring our whole selves to the table, with all our dreams, quirks, and the boisterous laughter we keep hushed at nice restaurants. I want us to be able to connect with one another, unashamed of who we are, or what we brought with us, or the things about us that might not be as shiny and perfect as we wish they were. I want us to know each other—deeply—and love each other anyway. Because that, my friends, is the cure to loneliness.

FRIENDSHIP CHANGES EVERYTHING

Many of the greatest gifts of my whole entire life are the women who fill it. I am surrounded by a group of women who know the worst things about me, who have seen me at the lowest points of my whole life, and who have loved me relentlessly through it all.

And my life is proof that love like that changes you.

There's nothing in the world like friendship. I am who I am, and am doing what I'm doing, unequivocally because of the women who have loved me throughout my life.

I recently got married, and while my favorite moment of the weekend was the, you know, actually getting married part, my other favorite moment of the weekend happened during our rehearsal dinner.

Carl, my husband, isn't a frequent crier. Although I've seen him tear up on several occasions, I'd never seen him actually cry, really cry, until this point.

He stood in front of our family and friends and gave a toast to my bridesmaids. He cried the whole way through, thanking them for making me the woman I am today. He thanked them for loving me, for teaching me, and for being there for me. The night before we got married, he made a point to recognize the women who have impacted me more deeply, more permanently than anyone else in my life.

Suffice it to say he wasn't the only one crying as he made that toast.

They say it takes a village to raise a child, but I think it takes a village to help us become the women we were always meant to be.

We need each other—a group of women to cook with, and go out with, and laugh with, and just do nothing with. We need women who will bring us dinner when something bad happens, or to answer our call at 4am to pray with us or tell us it's going to be okay. We need women who will help us paint the spare bedroom, or pick out a pair of shoes, or help us make sense of our wild and messy lives.

We need people who are like warm blankets in their comfort and peace, and people who tell us the truth, and shake us out of our mess when we need a strong word from someone who truly knows us. We need to be loved at our best, and at our worst by people who are standing next to us, fighting alongside us as we become our best selves.

We need each other. We need to be a team. We need people who are our people. We need a village.

SO WHERE DO WE GET THESE KINDS OF FRIENDSHIPS?

Depending on who you are and what your friendships have been like to this point, you may be thinking something along the lines of, "That's great for you. I'd love friendships like that. But it just hasn't happened for me." You may be taking inventory of the people in your life and feeling like the list is sparse—an unwelcome reminder that you don't have these kinds of friendships. I hear you.

All of us are going to come at this journey a little differently. Some of us have wonderful friends, all in the same place, just down the road, and available for an impromptu dinner party, or a good cry when needed.

Some of us have never had a village. We've tried to connect with other women but found ourselves hurt, rejected, or disappointed when the friendships didn't turn out as deep or committed as we thought they would.

Maybe you just moved (like I did recently), and left your village behind. Maybe you've found yourself crying to your husband because you miss your people so much, going on friend dates with perfect strangers in an effort to create a new community. Or maybe that's just me.

Maybe you have lots of friends, but they all hover somewhere around the surface. Maybe despite the fact that your calendar and Facebook is packed with acquaintances and invitations, you still feel incredibly lonely.

No matter how you got here, this isn't where we're going to stay. I'm going to take you on a journey into the life-long, life-changing friendships we all so desperately need. Are you with me? I hope so!

HOW WILL THIS GUIDE HELP?

Like I mentioned earlier, I got married just a few months ago, and my husband and I couldn't wait for our honeymoon. We dreamed about lots of places to go, and I slipped in the word "Europe" as often as possible. I was trying to be subtle, until he reminded me of the millions of other tourists with the same brilliant idea, and how hot it would be in the middle of the summer. Touché sir, I'll take a raincheck.

We spent weeks scouring the web for honeymoon locations until we found a resort in the Dominican Republic that had among its many luxuries, a pillow menu. Yes, a menu featuring various styles and varieties of pillows. Let's be honest, you can't just pass up a pillow menu.

Also, Carl's brother happens to be an accomplished diver and had mentioned that the DR is known for their scuba diving. He went over Christmas and couldn't stop raving about it. So on Zack's recommendation (and because of the pillow menu), to the Dominican Republic we went!

To be honest, I was hoping Carl would forget about that scuba diving thing. I was hoping he'd get so tied up in napping on the beach, eating, and other important activities that he would forget his desire for the depths altogether.

No such luck.

Now would be a good time to mention the fact that I'm semi-afraid of fish. I know they can't hurt me, (most of them). But I also know that I have little to zero desire to meet them face to face, or to be surrounded by them on their turf (as opposed to when they're in an aquarium and I'm peering in at them from the outside with a latte in hand).

Everything about scuba diving felt foreign and uncomfortable, and I was nervous about it from the minute he said he wanted to go. But knowing that I had been his wife for about 5 minutes by then, and not wanting to push my luck (just kidding, I just wanted to make him happy), I agreed.

So if you haven't scuba dived before, there's a whole process you have to go through before you actually do it. We didn't get certified, but we still went through a class, took a written test, and practiced in the pool before we ever got nose to nose with any fish.

The video was terrifying. In Spanish and English they described all the bad things that could happen to us if we weren't careful. If we didn't adhere to a ridiculously long list of rules, our ears could explode, our lungs could explode, any number of things could explode and it felt like a fine line between having it be a great day and having it be our last.

Once we'd gone into the pool and learned how to use our gear, they put us on a boat and took us out into the ocean. They dropped anchor and one by one, had us hop out of the boat and into the water—which is much easier said than done when you have that much weight strapped to your back and waist. We looked a bit like beached whales being rolled back into the ocean.

We floated in the water like awkwardly shaped buoys, until our instructor took our hands one by one and led us to the anchor's rope. He showed us how to grab onto the rope, and mimed from behind his scuba mask that we should climb our way down. So hand under hand, we followed him down the rope and to the bottom of the ocean. It was so comforting to have something to hold onto.

That's what I want this workbook to be for you. Exposing the depths of your heart to people you don't know super well might sound as fun to you as a trip to the dentist. You might be breaking out into a cold sweat already at the thought of such vulnerability. I totally hear you. But let this workbook be your rope — something to hold onto along the way. Let it be a constant reminder that there's a plan, and a promise that we'll get somewhere spectacular if you just stick with me.

When we made it to the bottom of the ocean, my frantic heartbeat started to slow, and the experience of sitting on the ocean floor is one I'll never forget. That day I learned that sometimes the scariest things are the most worthwhile, and I know journey this will be the same way.

So hand under hand we go. Grasp on, and get ready.

As you begin to remove some layers, you'll be well on your way to creating your village. And just like with scuba diving, our destination will be so worth the courage the journey required.

Are you ready to get started?

LET'S TALK LOGISTICS

How will this work exactly?

The long and short of it is that I'll be asking you questions. Each week we're talking about something different and the questions and topics get progressively deeper. Someone will need to read the introduction out loud (there's just something more communal about doing it that way), and then you'll dive into the questions.

You can either read the questions aloud one by one and answer them immediately, or give yourselves a few minutes to scan through them first. After each question I've given you some space to write notes. If you're the kind of person that needs to think through their answer first, this space is for you. It's also a good place to record your thoughts for later — a way of documenting the journey so you can look back and see how far you've come.

How you answer them is entirely up to you. You can do it discussion style, jumping in with your two cents whenever the person before you is done. Or you can go around in a circle, sharing one at a time. I'm a fan of the circle method over the "go whenever you feel like its your turn" method, just because I know when to be prepared, and then you avoid that awkward "do you want to go, or should I? dance" (Is it just me that hates that?)

How long should each question take?

It's up to your group and depends on how much time you've allotted for your time together. Regardless of how much time you have, it's helpful to have someone keeping an eye on the clock. The questions get deeper as we go, and I don't want you to skip the last ones for the sake of time. Also, if you're anything like me and my girlfriends, you could spend a year on the first question if left to your own devices. Set a time limit so you get through them all and aren't up all night.

Any tips or guidelines?

As people are talking, my humble request is that you give them your full, undivided attention. Put your phones on silent and stick them in your bag. Keep side conversations to a minimum and just listen. The things you'll be sharing in these weeks are intimate, and often scary. And there's nothing worse than sharing your deepest and darkest while someone is texting or checking their watch.

The other thing I'll ask of you is total safety. It's impossible (and foolish) to open up to people who aren't going to guard and protect the tender things you're sharing with them. So before you begin, I want you all to commit to keeping what's said in the group private, and being kind, and gentle with the things each woman shares. Safety is key in creating deep friendships, and so we have to start there.

What do the bonus questions mean?

After you're done with the questions each week, you'll find two bonuses below. The first says, "Stop and Smell the Roses," and the second says, "Go a Little Deeper…"

"Stop and Smell the Roses" is a place for you to reflect. So often we blaze through experiences and moments without taking the time to notice the beauty unfolding right before our eyes. I find that when I do take a moment to stop and notice, the world and what's happening in front of me becomes a kaleidoscope of color—showing me dimension and brilliance I didn't notice at first glance.

This section is a chance for you to reflect on what happened that week, a way to notice and remember the beautiful things you just watched unfold.

"Go a Little Deeper" is optional, but I highly recommend it. It's a challenge, a dare to take this to the next level, to be bold in the friendships you're creating and to make them even richer.

Tips for next week's meeting.

Before you end for the night, it's always a good idea to talk about next week's meeting, making sure everyone knows the time and the place. The weeks go progressively deeper, and this works best when everyone is fully committed and present each time. So take a minute before you leave to sync your calendars, and you'll be good to go!

With that, I think you're ready! Go ahead and keep reading. Week 1's questions are right around the corner.

NOTES

NOTES

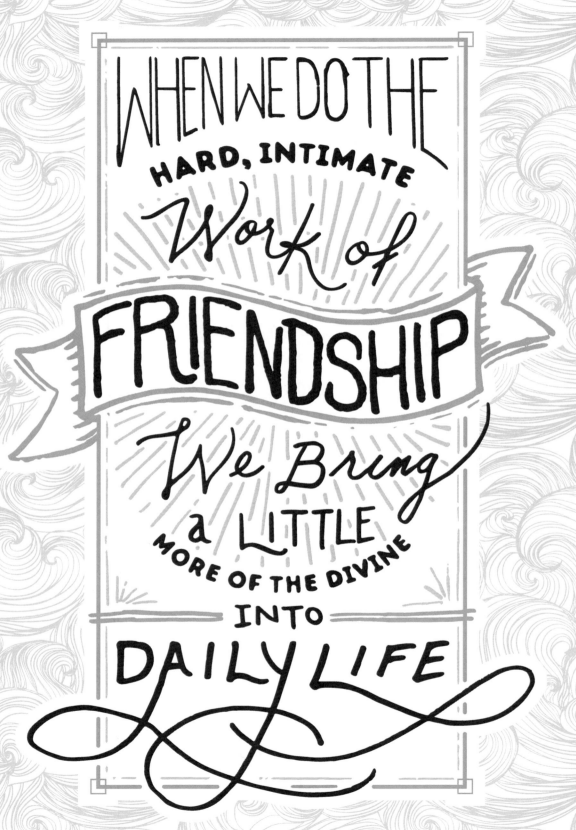

WHEN WE DO THE HARD, INTIMATE *Work of* FRIENDSHIP *We Bring* a LITTLE MORE OF THE DIVINE INTO DAILY LIFE

SHAUNA NIEQUIST

FRIENDSHIPS
& FRENEMIES

A big, official welcome to week one! I'm so happy you're here! I feel like I am (or rather wish I was) welcoming you into my home, hurrying into the kitchen to get a drink in your hand or some food in your belly.

I love bringing people together. It makes me so happy to think about each one of you gathering together, and about the love and connection that's going to multiply throughout the next six weeks.

We're about to jump in and get started, but before we do, I have just one last request of you.

BE BRAVE

There may be times over the next six weeks when this doesn't feel easy. There might be times when it feels much easier to keep your mouth shut, to keep your story to yourself, or even to stay home, and watch another episode of House Hunters.

I feel that every time I'm a part of a committed group activity. Whether it's a small group situation or an event, the idea of small talk and having to be "on" can be exhausting. My couch begins beckoning, and then come the excuses.

It's also really tempting to keep our thoughts and our words to ourselves. It's easier not to tell your story. It's less embarrassing if you don't risk crying in front of the group. It's safer to let people think you've got it all together, that you don't struggle with that, or worry about that, or feel insecure about that.

Telling your story and letting people get to know you—the real you—is the bravest thing you can do. And that's what I'm asking you to do today.

It's not safe, and it won't feel safe. It will feel uncomfortable and wild and like you want to crawl back into your shell.

But I'm going to ask you not to. I'm going to ask you to risk it. I'm going to ask you to keep going, to dig into what we're starting here, and to see what can happen when you actually let the women around you get to know the real you.

So be brave. For the next six weeks, be brave with the women around you. Share your story; say what you really think and feel, what really happened, and what you're really worried about. Then watch what happens. I promise it'll be miraculous.

So that's the favor I'm asking of you. No big deal, right? ;-)

FRIENDSHIPS & FRENEMIES

Without further ado, lets get going with Week 1. Week 1 is all about friendship: past, present, and future. We're starting here because we need to lay the foundation for where we're going.

As women, friendship is a tricky thing. It evokes a thousand different images, and emotions for each of us. For some of us, the word brings about memories of slumber parties and life-long companions. It's a happy word, a warm word, a connected word. For others of us, the word "friendship" carries memories of mean girls, and backstabbing, of being left out, or simply lonely.

None of us have the same experiences or foundations with friendship, and that's why I want to start here today. It's time to get real with each other about where we come from in our female friendships. If we don't know where we each come from, we'll have no idea how to approach each other. We need to know what we've all been through, what we've experienced when it comes to friendships, what's worked and what hasn't.

A few years ago I made a friend who I just couldn't figure out. We had tons in common, lots of things to talk about, and shared experiences to discuss. But for the longest time we were never able to go deep in our friendship. It was like there was a thick piece of glass between the two of us and nothing I did was able to remove it. I couldn't get her to open up, couldn't dive deep, couldn't seem to gain her trust. I thought I was doing something wrong for a long, long time, until I found out she'd been had terrible experiences with female friendships in the past. It wasn't about me at all! Once I understood where she was coming from, we were able to build something beautiful. To this day, she's one of my closest friends, but we had to start out on the same page.

Let's get started!

WEEK 1 QUESTIONS:

Tell us about the closest friend you've ever had. What made that friendship so close and special?

_____

_____

_____

_____

_____

What do you value most in friendships? What do you look for in a friend?

_____

_____

_____

_____

_____

What is going through your mind as you're meeting new women? (Do you have an open heart or a guarded one? What thoughts are you thinking about them, and what thoughts are you thinking about yourself?)

_____

_____

_____

_____

_____

What's the worst experience you've ever had with a female friendship?

_____

_____

_____

_____

_____

What holds you back from investing deeply in friendships?

_____

_____

_____

_____

_____

What kinds of friendships do you have in your life today, and what kinds would you like more of?

_____

_____

_____

_____

_____

Thank you so much for answering with such bravery and honesty. I'm so glad we started here, because this is the foundation. We have to know where we're starting before we can get to where we're going.

Not only is this great practice for opening up and getting to know each other, but I hope it's also a great reminder that even the people you think have more best friends than they know what to do with sometimes feel lonely and disconnected. Everyone could use more connection in their lives, and it takes a whole lot of honesty and bravery to admit that out loud. With that foundation under our feet, we can now begin to build.

I'm so proud of you for your courage, and for showing up here tonight. I know we're only at the beginning, but I hope you can look at the women around you and feel like you know them a bit more deeply than you did when you walked in the door.

Keep going, make this a priority, and stay in it. You'll be amazed what happens when you stick this out for six weeks with the women around your table.

The last thing I want you to do is pray together. Have someone pray for the group, for all the things you just shared, and that God would bless the friendships you're creating here. I know He will.

And with all my love, and gratitude for you showing up here tonight, I'm sending you on your way!

Have a wonderful night, don't forget to set the date and time for your next meeting, and I'll see you next week!

All my love,

Stephanie

P.S. Your bonuses are on the next page!

Stop and smell the roses:

_____

_____

_____

_____

_____

Go a little deeper:

This week, I dare you to start a group text. It can be a place where you share stories, links to great articles, fun things that have happened during the week, and even prayer requests. Having that consistent communication—even via text—is a great way to take friendships deeper one day at a time.

NOTES

NOTES

FRIENDSHIP IS BORN
AT THAT MOMENT WHEN
ONE MAN SAYS TO ANOTHER

what?!
you too?

I THOUGHT I WAS
THE ONLY ONE.

C.S. LEWIS

LESSONS IN LOVE

Hi sweet friends! Welcome back!

Today we're talking about our romantic relationships. It seems like such a girly topic, doesn't it? It seems like one of those things women are supposed to get together and gossip about, over nail polish and brownies. Having an aversion to all things cliché, I almost skipped it entirely, but then I had a change of heart.

I've always felt silly that this was the case, but my story is threaded through with relationships. Good ones, bad ones, no one, and the right one have all shepherded me from one place to the next, teaching me, growing me, and moving me along my way.

I always used to wish I could learn lessons in different, more intellectual ways, but nope. My heart has always been the epicenter of my lesson learning. The path to who I am today has been paved and guided by some spectacular, and not so spectacular, men.

Relationships can bring out the best parts of us, and the worst parts of us. They break us open and reveal our vulnerability like nothing else can. I want to talk about relationships because who you've loved, and who you've lost can have such an impact on your formation as a person and on your view of yourself.

Something I'm learning now more than ever is that everyone is going through something. Even the women we think have it all together are struggling with something, and I think if we knew that, we'd feel much less alone.

I have friends who are single, who have never really dated anybody, and who are wrestling through what that means and how they view themselves as a result. It's hard to watch everyone around you get married and to not wonder if something might be wrong with you—if there's some reason you're not doing the same.

I have friends who are dating, who are wondering if they're dating the right guy, if they should move forward in their relationship, or if he'll ever, EVER propose.

I have friends who are going through a breakup. They're waking up every day hoping the ache in their chest will subside just a bit, making it a little easier to breathe, and the corners of their mouth a little less heavy, able to turn up into a smile again.

I have friends who are engaged—who are navigating the tricky waters of combining two lives and two families, of planning a wedding, and all of the life change that surrounds that big day.

I have friends, like myself, who have just gotten married. They're navigating all the wonderfully strange things that come with combining your life with a boy—from setting up your first place, to merging your finances, to sex, to what it means to be a good wife.

And I have friends who have been married for a long time who are still wondering if they're doing it right, and why other people's marriages seem to be easier, smoother, or happier than their own.

This is so often how we feel. It's easy for us to look around at everyone else and think we're the only ones who don't have perfect relationships. It's easy for us to think we're the only ones who ever get mad for no reason, or feel like we may just be a little too messed up to make this work. We sometimes feel unwanted or insecure, and whether you're single or married, I know we've all felt that way.

My best friends Kelsey and Michelle and I have learned a lot about friendship's role in relationships recently. We've walked each other through more breakups than I can count, and have helped each other nurse our hearts back to health. But the one phase of life we've never been in together until recently is the phase where we're all seriously dating someone or getting married. That's something different altogether.

Kelsey got engaged right after me, and her wedding was 7 weeks after ours. Michelle is engaged to a truly spectacular guy. All of us are learning new and different things about how relationships work, and who we are within them. Something we realized a while ago is that it's really easy to compare one relationship to another.

I would glance over at Kelsey and her husband, and think, "They would never fight about something this stupid. I wish our relationship were more like theirs." Or I'd look at Michelle and her fiancé and think of all the things her relationship had that ours didn't. But what we discovered (after some frustrating and comparison-filled months) was that they were doing the same with me!

We were all navigating the ins and outs of relationships, but we were only discussing the happy things. Without any truth or reality, comparison went nuts! All three of us were left wondering if we were the only ones who got in stupid fights sometimes, or if we were the only ones without a perfect relationship. We were comparing our imperfectly wonderful relationships to relationships we knew very little about. We always came up short. It was the worst!

And so in a decisive moment, we changed all of that. We began sharing the real things that were going on, just like we always had in other parts of our lives, but had forgotten about for a while. We started telling each other about the disagreements, or asking for comfort or prayer or wisdom on a day when we were feeling unwanted or insecure for no particular reason.

When we started being honest with each other about where we were, and just how not-perfect our lives are, we realized we were all in the boat together.

Nobody's lives or relationships are perfect. Not a one. No matter where we are on the relationship continuum, every single one of us feels insecure, worries that we're going to mess everything up, and stays up at night wondering if how we're feeling is normal.

When we all can be honest about those things, and tell the stories of what's really going on in our lives, the façade begins to erode. We can see that we're all just people trying to navigate life, and all doing it super imperfectly. There is nothing in the world more comforting than that.

That's why we're here today. We're here to dispel some of those myths, to talk about where we are really, and to find out that we're not alone.

All of us have doubts, fears, insecurities, and worries when it comes to our romantic relationships. It's time we realized we're not the only one and we can be in this together. Are you ready?

WEEK 2 QUESTIONS:

What do you enjoy most about where you are in relationships today?
(Single, dating, married, divorced, widowed, etc.)

_____

_____

_____

_____

_____

What's the hardest part about it? What are you wrestling with right now?

_____

_____

_____

_____

_____

Think back over your romantic history. What events from that past make the greatest impact on your relationships or singleness today? (Ex. a particular breakup, something someone said to you once, losing someone, something that you've seen in your parents' marriage, etc.)

_____

_____

_____

_____

_____

What are you learning about relationships right now?

_____

_____

_____

_____

_____

How can we as a group support you in your romantic relationships?

_____

_____

_____

_____

_____

Relationships are one of the most beautiful, most important, most gut-wrenching parts of our lives. Romance is the area where our brains seem to shut down, and our hearts seem to go into overdrive. In other words, we could use some help.

Luckily, that's what we're here to provide. We're here to cultivate a group of friends who can be there to help you, and your current or potential spouse, along the way.

Think about the concept of bridesmaids. Let's be honest, they're not just up there for the dresses. They're standing next to you promising they'll help you along the way. Their presence is a silent promise that they'll answer your phone call in the middle of the night, they'll talk some sense into you when you sorely need it, and they'll come over with an extra large pizza and a movie when something has gone wrong.

This is what you can be for each other. Look around you. This group can be a support system, a sounding board, a safe place with wise words of advice, ready to offer perspective, help, or even just a listening ear.

We're in this together, if we choose to be. And I hope we do, because relationships have enough pressure to them without thinking everyone else's are perfect. And I'm so much better to Carl when I have the support, love and wisdom of my best friends backing me up.

I know your relationships will be so much better too.

Take a moment and pray together for all the relationships, past, present, and future, that you shared about today.

Have a wonderful week!

All my love,

Stephanie

Stop and smell the roses:

_____

_____

_____

_____

_____

Go a little deeper:

This week, I dare you to get coffee with a girl in the group. Be bold, get each other's numbers and head out someplace cute for a cup of something delicious. I want these friendships to start to pop right off the page, and expand past what you're doing on the days when you meet.

NOTES

I DO NOT UNDERSTAND THE MYSTERY OF *grace* ONLY THAT IT MEETS US WHERE WE ARE & DOES NOT LEAVE US WHERE IT FOUND US

ANNE LAMOTT

REAL TALK
ON FAITH

Well hello sweet friends!

Welcome to week three!

I want you to take a second and reflect on where we've been. Look at the women around your table, or around your living room, or whatever little corner of the world you meet in. Think about how well you knew them when we started, and all that's happened in the last two weeks.

Think of the bravery that's been shown, and the courage people have displayed as they've revealed pieces of their story that weren't easy to share.

I always like to pause for a second and take stock of what's changed. Otherwise I get so caught up in what I'm doing I forget there's been any progress at all.

But there has been progress. You have been meeting together for three weeks today, and that's a big deal!

This week we're going to talk about faith. This is one of my favorite things to talk about with my girlfriends because it is another one of those things that can feel so isolating and confusing when we're going at it alone.

I don't know if it's ever felt this way for you. But sometimes our Christian friends and our normal friends seem to be two different things. They're opposing forces almost, like pushing the same side of a magnet together.

In college, I know that felt like the case. I had my "good" friends—the rule followers, the ones I saw on Tuesday nights at church. But they weren't the ones I actually spent time with. Not really.

Then I had my other friends. They were the wild ones, the rule breakers for sure. They had nothing to do with my faith, but I spent most of my time with them. Then I'd wonder why faith seemed so darn hard.

When I finally became real, honest to goodness friends with some incredible Christians, everything changed for me. Life was no longer segmented. I wasn't a different person on Tuesday nights than I was the rest of the week, and the rest of my nights didn't seem so different from the life I was trying to start living.

We find friends in lots of places, and it's great to have all kinds. But there's nothing I've found to be more helpful and impactful for my faith than great friends who also believed the same things I did. It made life, faith, and becoming who I wanted to be so much easier.

Not only are we going to talk about faith today, but we're going to talk about our doubts as well.

It's an unpopular thing to admit when you have doubts about God, but I think you'll soon discover we all do.

Several months ago, I was sitting around chatting with a group of friends. We hadn't talked in a while, so our conversation was full of the top stories in our lives, catching each other up. There was a lull in the conversation when all of a sudden one of the girls dove in and said one of the most beautifully honest things I'd heard in a long time.

"I suck at being a Christian!"

She almost yelled it, the honesty pushing up and out of her like a sneeze.

And when she said it, we all burst out laughing.

A chorus of "me too" rang around that room, because we knew exactly what she was talking about.

None of us had been stellar about reading our Bibles, or making it to church every single Sunday. None of us had been giving God the time and attention we wanted to, and we all felt like the others would judge us if they knew. That was until one brave friend spoke up and gave us all the permission to do the same. We were all a mess, all imperfect, and we were in it together.

Deep breath.

Our group of friends changed that day. We were no longer people who expected each other to know what we were doing or maintain the façade of having it together. We were all figuring it out and we didn't have to do it alone.

That's what I want us to do this week. I want us to admit the things that we usually keep to ourselves—the doubts we're pretty sure nobody else has, the questions we're afraid to ask. If you can't ask them here, where can you ask them? So I hope you ask them here.

WEEK 3: QUESTIONS

Tell us about your experience with faith/the church growing up

_____

_____

_____

_____

_____

Do you have a relationship with God now? If so, when did it start? If not, what's holding you back?

_____

_____

_____

_____

_____

When were you the angriest with God?

_____

_____

_____
_____
_____

What's one really great thing you've seen come out of the Christian Church?

_____
_____
_____
_____
_____

What's something you've seen the Christian Church do that you didn't like?

_____
_____
_____
_____
_____

What doubt do you have that you rarely admit to people? (About church, God, or Christianity).

_____
_____
_____
_____
_____

What is God teaching you today?

_____

_____

_____

_____

_____

To finish up this week, I want you to get into pairs to pray with one other person.

I don't know about you, but so often I find myself needing things that I just don't have the words to pray for. Especially when it comes to my relationship with God, I sometimes feel like my prayers fall flat, and it's so helpful to have someone else praying for me when I need some backup.

We were never meant to walk this path alone, especially in our faith.

Have a wonderful week!

All my love,

Stephanie

Stop and smell the roses:

_____

_____

_____

_____

_____

Go a little deeper:

This week I dare you to go to church with another member of your group.
Maybe you all decide to go together for one week, to try out a new church, or
return to an old one. Maybe you decide to go back to church for the first time
in a long time. It doesn't have to be permanent, there's no pressure attached. It's
just a way for you to experience and learn something together.

NOTES

NOTES

I NOW SEE HOW

OWNING OUR STORY

& LOVING OURSELVES

THROUGH THAT PROCESS

IS THE BRAVEST THING

THAT WE WILL EVER DO.

BRENE BROWN

IF YOU ONLY KNEW MY FAMILY...

Hi friends!

Welcome back for week four! I'm so glad you're here, because I've been really looking forward to our topic tonight.

Tonight we're talking about our families.

Now, some of you may have felt nothing when you heard me say that, but others of you may have just felt your stomachs drop all the way to the floor.

That variety of reactions is why we're bringing this up tonight: Our families, for better or for worse, have a major impact on who we are today. Much of how we see the world, ourselves in it, love, and sex, and marriage, having kids, and the difference we can make in the world can be traced back to how we grew up. And that's why I want to talk about it today.

For many of you, no matter how your life looked growing up, you might find some of your most trying and frustrating relationships right there in your family. I've heard so many people say that they feel like they're a good person until this one member of their family does that one certain thing, and then all bets are off.

I know I've felt this way with my mom. The poor woman has loved me to pieces my entire life. But something about our relationship has this way of pulling out all of the ugly that was stored up in my heart, and exploding it all over her. It's been quite the journey to learn to treat her with the love she deserves, and it's one my friends have had a major hand in.

Like anything else in life, the ins and outs of family are easier when we have some love and support backing us up. That's why I want us to share our families, and our stories with each other today.

Here's the other thing: For some of us, really ugly things have happened to us as a result of our families. The subject of our families, their legacies, the things we've inherited from them, and the things they've done to us are often the source of great shame and isolation in our lives.

When something really bad has happened to you, that thing might be the lynchpin to you feeling known. It might be that thing that you keep locked so tightly inside of you that keeps you from being close to the people around you. It might be that thing you keep as such a secret because you're afraid that when other people find out what happened, they'll leave.

This group isn't meant to be therapy, and it won't replace it, certainly. But this group can be a listening ear, allowing you to come forward with the things you usually carry on your shoulders alone, allowing you to set it down for a while.

I hope you take the leap to open up about that thing tonight—whether something really bad happened, you have a really tough relationship with a family member, or there are just things you'd like to see go differently in your family when you have one, I want us to talk about those things.

Our families have a major impact on who we are, for better or for worse, and I think if we're really going to get to know and trust each other, talking about our families is a major step.

WEEK 4: QUESTIONS

Give us a rundown on your family: Siblings? Parents? Are they married or divorced? Etc.

_____

_____

_____

_____

_____

What is one thing your family has done well that you'd want to repeat in your own family?

_____

_____

_____

_____

_____

What is something your family has done poorly that you wouldn't want to repeat?

_____

_____

_____

_____

_____

Which is your hardest familial relationship, and why?

_____

_____

_____

_____

_____

What is one situation/incident from your family history that impacts the way you live your daily life?

_____

_____

_____

_____

_____

How can the women around this table help you love your family better?

_____

_____

_____

_____

_____

Thank you so much for opening up to each other. Talking about our families, the dynamics within them, and the things that have happened in our lives is not easy. But I hope you're looking around at people who feel much closer because of the things they just shared with you, and the way they cared for you when you were the one sharing.

To end tonight, I want to spend some time in prayer for yourselves and for your families. Lead it however you feel is best, whatever you need to finish out the night, but prayer is powerful and I would love for all of your families to be the beneficiaries of your prayers tonight.

All my love and I'll see you next week!

Stephanie

Stop and smell the roses:

_____

_____

_____

_____

_____

Go a little deeper:

This week I dare you to pray for another member of the group's family. Think about the things she shared tonight and spend time praying for them this week. You can tell her that you're praying, or you don't have to. But either way, when we pray for someone, our relationships deepen.

NOTES

YOU ARE
IMPERFECT,
PERMANENTLY
& INEVITABLY
flawed.
AND YOU ARE
Beautiful

-AMY BLOOM

AN ATTACK ON OUR OWN WORST CRITICS

A few years ago, I was on a weekend retreat with a group of girlfriends. We all knew each other, certainly, but we weren't best friends, not soul-mate best friends, at least not all of us.

We'd had a long few months of work and needed some time to refuel, and so in the most relaxing, most delicious weekend, we ate fresh-made pasta, drank exquisite wine, and spent lots of time by the pool and at the beach.

When I left that weekend, my heart felt like it was full to overflowing, but it wasn't because of the wine or because of the pasta, or even because of the beach, if you can believe it.

The thing that filled me up so entirely was a conversation we all had while sitting at an outdoor cafe one afternoon.

I couldn't tell you how we got on the subject, because I truly don't remember. I don't remember who spoke first, or how we got around to confessing the things we did that day. All I know is I came out of that conversation with the profound knowledge that in one of the deepest, toughest, most rampant areas of fear and insecurity in my life, I am simply not alone.

We all have tapes that play in our heads. They're like scratched CDs, repeating the same messages over and over in our minds. The messages come from a lot of places. An experience teaches us something, or maybe it's something someone said. But somewhere along the line we begin believing things about ourselves, and often-times the things we believe aren't the best.

We become our own worst critic, a mean, condescending voice in our head telling us all the things that are wrong with us. "You're fat," it tells us as we catch a glimpse of our reflection. Or "I can't believe you said that, you really shouldn't talk anymore," when we've worked up the nerve to speak our minds. "You're too much, not enough, ugly, have weird hair. You're not a nice person, you're a lot of work, you're high maintenance…"

There are things we believe to be true about ourselves that we may not even realize, yet those cruel voices keep us from ever feeling good enough, or ever feeling truly loved.

For some of us, our worst insecurities are physical. We grew up as a bigger kid in a stick-thin family, or learned early that we should be embarrassed by a birthmark, or our nose, or our teeth.

For others of us, our worst insecurities are internal—personality traits we quickly learned are "not okay." There are things about us that should be hidden, downplayed, or covered up completely.

The worst part is that we believe we're the only ones who feel this way, the only ones who are torn to shreds by the thoughts inside our heads.

We look at the confident, beautiful women around us convinced that they don't struggle the way we do. "They couldn't possibly feel insecure or have anything to be ashamed of."

But the truth is, we all do. We all have things that make us feel small—traits, quirks, or ideas about ourselves that make us feel unattractive or too messy to love. And when we finally can admit those to each other, we can realize that we're in this together. There is no one who feels perfect, or who doesn't battle with their thoughts.

And the best part about being honest about those insecurities, is that we can begin to fight them together.

So that day at the sidewalk cafe, we went around the circle admitting the things about ourselves we just can't stand. For one girl, it was a birthmark on her neck. We squinted and cocked our heads to one side, and then the other, but we could barely see it, and definitely couldn't understand why she was so freaked out about it. Yet it kept her wearing chunky necklaces, and scarves, just so no one would see it.

For another girl, it was her exuberant personality. She'd always believed she was a lot to handle, more than anyone would really want. She tried to keep herself quiet, and had taught herself to fade into the background when she'd obviously been created to stand out.

We admitted the things that made us feel embarrassed, or small, or not good enough, and we each had something. But there was a consistency in that circle—a pattern we began to notice. Not one of the things these beautiful women had spent so long worrying about took anything away from the beauty we saw sitting in front of us. We had never noticed the things the others were so insecure about. We had never considered that they were too loud, or too much. We had never seen the birthmark. And even when they brought attention to these things, we almost had to laugh because they were so tiny, so ridiculously insignificant compared to the amazing qualities we saw in one another.

At the end of the conversation, we spent time telling each woman what she actually looked like. With our words, we brought her to a mirror and helped her see the truth about who she really is. We pointed out gifts, and strengths, and beauty she couldn't see on her own. That afternoon was a major blow to our internal critics, and the beginning of a beautiful journey of self acceptance and even love.

We walked away from that conversation feeling a thousand pounds lighter, and a thousand times closer to each other. We had let someone else hear the tapes in our head, and had a whole group fighting with us to silence them. We felt deeply known and freer than we had in as long as any of us could remember. It was glorious.

So that's what we're doing today, we're going to confess our insecurities, both internal and external, and then we're going to fight back against them together.

Be bold with each other. If you are, I know that whatever that thing is—whatever makes you feel unworthy of love, or ugly, or like you have to hide—will lose so much of its power over you.

None of us are perfect, and we are all incredibly beautiful. I hope this time helps you see that a bit more clearly.

TWO QUICK TIPS:

1. Don't fight against the lies quite yet

As you're listening to each other, you're going to be tempted to jump in, to fight for your friends against the mean thoughts their minds have been throwing at them. But wait. There will be a time when we can fight for each other, and when we can refute all of these negative, heartbreaking thoughts we believe about ourselves. But for now, and while we're answering the questions, let's allow each other to have a moment with our own thoughts. There's such power in realizing what thoughts we actually think about ourselves, and only when we acknowledge those thoughts can we really be helped by the truth others tell us. So for now, do your very best to just listen and let each other process.

2. Watch your body language

As you're listening, be very careful and cognizant of your body language and your reactions. When you're admitting something scary to a group, having someone innocently laugh or look at their watch while you're talking can feel like a stab to the heart. Keep your phones away, keep your eyes on the person who's speaking, and minimize any side conversations. That will help the person feel extra safe as they're opening up to you.

WEEK 5: QUESTIONS

What's your favorite aspect of both your physical appearance and heart/personality?

_____

_____

_____

_____

_____

What parts of yourself (both outside and inside) do you spend the most time trying to fix or to hide?

_____

_____

_____

_____

_____

How do you try to hide these things? How does this insecurity impact your daily life, or decisions?

_____

_____

_____

_____

_____

What do you worry will happen if people notice these "flaws" in you?

_____

_____

_____

_____

_____

If these insecurities disappeared (if you learned to accept them, or even love them), how would your life be different?

_____

_____

_____

_____

_____

What tangible steps would you need to take to make it so this insecurity no longer has power over you?

_____

_____

_____

_____

_____

Now it's time to fight back.

Each of you has a piece of paper in your guide. It's a gorgeous sketch of a woman's profile, drawn by one of my very best friends, Amanda.

I want you to write your name on the top of your sheet, and pass your book to the right. Now, with the new notebook you have in front of you, you are that person's note-taker. Your job is to write down everything people say about them.

Now, one by one, I want each of you to spend a few minutes in the "hot seat." And then I want the rest of the group to go around and tell you what they see when they look at you. This can be a combination of personality traits, gifts, skills, and physical attributes.

When it's your turn to sit in the hot seat, try to relax and listen to the things the women around you are saying. Your note taker will be writing down every word for you to keep and look at later.

We're harsh with ourselves; with no help from anyone else we have the ability to make ourselves feel so small. Sometimes it takes the eyes of people who love us to show us what we really look like.

I hope that's what you do for each other.

When you're done, and when you walk away from this time, I hope you can see yourselves in a new light—through the eyes of people who love you. And when you need a reminder, you have this beautiful print with the truth about who you are scrawled all over it. I hope you frame it and put it up somewhere where you can see it—where those words, and praises can sink into your skin, becoming the new tapes playing on repeat in your mind.

NOTES

NOTES

A dream
you dream alone
is only a dream

A dream you
dream together
& is reality.

john lennon

SHE WILL MOVE MOUNTAINS

Hi sweet friends!

This is our very last week and I can't wait for today's topic.

Today we're talking about our dreams, about the things that are on our minds and hearts, the things we want to create and accomplish in the world.

The reason we're talking about this now is because our dreams point so clearly to who we are, and who we want to be. When we share these with each other, we're inviting a band of girlfriends to come behind and beside us, enabling us to travel further, and making the journey infinitely more fun.

Like I said before, I am where I am because of the girlfriends who helped and encouraged me along the way. I want that to be true for you as well. I also want you to experience the intimacy that comes when we share our deepest desires with each other. I know you'll be amazed.

Just like friendships, we're all going to come at this a little differently. Some of us know precisely what we dream of doing. Some of us have no idea. Most of us are somewhere in between. Maybe you're approaching college graduation and feel an immense pressure to know exactly what you're going to do with your life. Maybe you're a mom of small children and you laughed out loud when I suggested you might have dreams for your life. (You do have dreams, they're just buried in piles of diapers, or lost between carpool trips and play-dates). Or maybe there's something you've always wanted to do but you never say out loud. It can be fun to imagine sometimes, but you've never considered the possibility of it actually happening.

I want you to suspend reality for a second. Close your eyes if you want to and picture yourself letting go of all the things that hold you back. Let go of the pressure to have a plan, of expectations and responsibilities. Let go of your busy schedule and all the reasons why your dream—whatever it is—could never work.

For right now, we're going to just dream.

So with your eyes closed, or leaning back into your chair, I'm going to ask you a few preliminary questions. This is just to get your wheels turning.

After you hear the questions, I want you to take a second and jot down some notes. Don't hold yourself back or allow your inner editor to give her two cents. Just write down whatever comes to mind.

Are you ready? Here are your preliminary questions.

What is the thing that keeps you up at night? The thing you could talk about for days and never ever get tired of?

What is the thing you find yourself researching absentmindedly, or the thing all the people you follow on Instagram are really, really good at?

What would you do if your schedule was suddenly empty, or if you never had to worry about paying your bills again?

What's the thing you make time for no matter what, the thing that keeps your mind clear and your heart full?

What's the dream you had as a child that lives somewhere in the back of your mind—appearing every once in a while just to remind you it's still there?

Now take a few minutes to write down what came to mind. Again, remind your inner editor that she's not welcome at this party.

_____

_____

_____

_____

_____

_____

_____

_____

_____

_____

You may feel silly as you look back on what you just wrote. But I'll kindly ask you not to. The things you wrote down aren't silly at all. They're important.

These things point to something—something you're uniquely wired to love, and to want, and I think those things have a lot, if not everything, to do with what we were made to do on this earth.

The other thing I believe is this: We need each other if we're going to make these things happen.

If you've ever chased a dream, you know it's not easy. It's daunting immediately. All of your shortcomings and reasons you are totally inadequate zoom to the forefront of your mind. You feel exposed, like rejection is surely lurking in the shadows just waiting to pounce.

But being on each others' team is like a secret weapon—something that makes us bigger and stronger than we could ever be on our own.

Without the support of my girlfriends I would never have had the courage to apply for that job, or that internship. I would never have had the security to start that blog, or to write a book. Their support felt like backup—like an army of troops behind me and on my side.

They're also endlessly helpful. They call me on random Tuesday afternoons with blog ideas, or crazy new products for my business. They pass out my book like candy in a parade—A book for you! A book for you! A book for you! They're fierce in their loyalty to me, and give the very best pep talks when I feel like giving up.

No matter what beautiful work is ours to do in the world, we can't do it alone. We need people on our team and beside us and that's what we're going to talk about today. We're going to bring our dreams together, offering suggestions and ways to help each other out. A rising tide raises all ships and we're going to see that phrase in action.

So let's get started!

A quick tip:

As you're listening to each other talk, look for connections between yourselves that might not be immediately obvious. If one of you loves to cook and another is passionate about makeup, there is absolutely a way to collaborate there. Get creative, think outside the box, help each other!

WEEK 6 QUESTIONS:

Start by telling everyone what you're doing right now. What does your day-to-day look like? What are you pursuing right now?

_____
_____
_____
_____
_____

Do you feel like you're on the right track? Is there something you'd like to do differently?

_____
_____
_____
_____
_____

If you could fix one problem or change one thing about the world, what would it be?

_____

_____

_____

_____

_____

What is a short-term dream or goal you have for yourself?

_____

_____

_____

_____

_____

What's the dream that's so big you're embarrassed to admit it out loud? Yes, I want you to admit it out loud. Quick hint: While it's so fun to have dreams that are totally beyond the realm of possibility (Mine is to be a pop-star. Too bad I'm not a great singer!) I want to instead talk about gigantic things that are terrifying, and hard to do, but still possible.

_____

_____

_____

_____

_____

What help do you need to make your dream happen?

_____

_____

_____

_____

_____

Now that everyone has shared, this is what I want you to do: One by one, I want you to go around the circle putting one woman and her dream, big or small, in the spotlight for a few minutes. While she's in the spotlight, I want the whole group to focus on her, and together, brainstorm ways you each can use your resources, your connections, your time, your talents, your job, and whatever else you have to support her.

A girlfriend of mine is a fantastic singer and actress that just moved to New York. I made sure to connect her with my uncle who is a play-write. You never know what connections could lead to. Even if it's just as simple as sharing someone's blog on your social media, think of anything you have that you could use to help each other achieve your dreams.

Do that for each woman in the circle, and when you're done, take a few minutes to pray as a group for the dreams you just discussed.

Here's some space to take notes during the brainstorm:

_____

_____

_____

_____

_____

_____

_____

_____

_____

_____

_____

_____

_____

_____

_____

_____

_____

_____

_____

_____

Lastly, I actually want you to do these things. This is a jumping off point into getting your hands messy in the dreams and lives of the women around this table.

It takes a village to help us become the women we were always mean to be, and this is where that happens. World changing women have a team behind them — cheering them on, helping them along the way, and picking them up when they fall down. We need each other if we're going to do the major things God has for us to do in this world. And the world needs us to do those things.

Stop and smell the roses:

_____

_____

_____

_____

_____

Go a little deeper:

This week, I dare you to take action in helping another woman in the group achieve her dream. Send the introductory email to help her make a connection, share her blog on your Facebook page, buy something from her Etsy shop. An incredible trust is built when we feel that people are advocating for us and on our team. And with us all working together, I can't imagine what we can accomplish!

NOTES

A TIME
TO REFLECT

We did it! We're done! But before we go, I want to take a second to reflect.

Too often we blaze from one thing to another before we take a second and realize what just happened, so that's what I want to do right now. First, I want you to remember back to what life looked like just six weeks ago. I want you to think about perceptions you had, fears you came in with, and worries you were lugging around like carry-on baggage.

Now look at the faces of each woman sitting around this table. Think about who you thought they were to begin with, and who you now know them to be. Think about the stories they've shared with you and the connections you've made.

Friendship is really important. It is. And as wonderful as our relationships with men are, our jobs, our kids, our homes, our hobbies, nothing can replace the unique need we all have for best friends.

You have started something profound here in the last six weeks. You've begun to be honest with a new group of women, or an old group of women in a new way. You've let people in, and let them get to know you, both the ugly parts and the beautiful parts. And I bet you anything that more beauty came through your admission of those ugly parts than ugly did.

You've grasped onto the rope, and you've gone to new depths together. I hope you continue investing in these friendships. I hope you keep making time in your schedules, and gathering over a meal. I fully believe that if you do, and if you continue asking each other the hard questions, and making the courageous confessions that bring about such beautiful, connective vulnerability, you will be radically changed by the friendship and the love that fills your life.

Female friendship is one of the most powerful, profound, and shaping things you have in your life, and I hope you make the most of it.

Don't let this be the end, make this the beginning. I can't wait to see what you accomplish together.

Thank you for trusting me and going on this journey with me. I'm truly honored to have spent these 6 weeks with you.

I'd love to hear any and all stories from you about how it went, and the connections that you made with each other. Please feel free to email me anytime. Stephanie@StephanieMayWilson.com

All my love,

Stephanie

Stop and smell the roses:

_____

_____

_____

_____

_____

Go a little deeper:

My dare for you on this last week is to add one more date on the calendar. Do it now before you forget, or before life gets away from you. It's a bonus week, Week 7 if you'll allow me. There's no curriculum, no questions to be answered, or ideas to delve into. Instead, I just want you to hang out. Make reservations at your favorite restaurant and have a girls' night together. Or make dinner at someone's house and laugh and just talk.

This is the most important part of the whole journey—the part where your friendships pop off the page and explode with color into your real, everyday life. Enjoy it, and make a toast: "To our new village!"

NOTES

TAKE IT A
STEP FURTHER

Just because this particular journey is over, doesn't mean
there aren't hundreds more to venture on together.

Here are a few ideas of how to connect now that you're finished:

- Start (or keep up with) a text message thread for your group. Share stories, prayer requests, thoughts, and daily updates! It's an easy, unobtrusive, but lovely way to connect throughout the day!

- Start a book club. Reading a book together is a wonderful chance for a common experience. Also, it's a great excuse to meet every few weeks and drink wine and eat great food together!

- Start a cooking club. Once a month (or however often works for you), gather at each other's houses and all bring a different dish. It's a fun way to connect regularly over a delicious (and low-stress) meal!

- Join a Bible Study together. It's always easier to join something new when you already know someone. This is a great way to not only stay in touch with these friends, but to connect to even more!

- Pray for each other. When we're praying for people, something just shifts. It's like we jump into their lives with them. It's a fantastic way to fight for your friends, to advocate for them, or just to support them.

- Introduce your boyfriends/husbands to each other. Now that you have a whole new set of friends, wouldn't it be great to include your significant others in the group? You never know what kind of friendships or connections could come from that!

- Start going to church together. Maybe you've been looking for a new church, or a new community to plug into. Why not team up with some of the women you just got to know? It's a great way of connecting to even more people, and beginning to establish the faith community you may have been searching for!

- Start a mastermind group. A mastermind group is a group of people who are all striving for a professional goal. It's like a long-term version of what we did in Week 2. It's a great way to make connections, to continue to work together, and to find awesome people to collaborate with.

Take a girl's getaway together! It doesn't have to be expensive, or even a long trip. Hop in the car, and drive somewhere fun where you can kick back and spend some restful time together.

Whatever you do next, remember that the more you invest in these friendships, the closer, and more connected you'll feel. It takes time, and consistency, but you will be so grateful and will gain so much from the investment you make.

HAVE FUN!

About Stephanie May Wilson

Stephanie May Wilson is equal parts writer and celebrator who believes that even Tuesday is worthy of a champagne toast. She believes in the healing power of a warm cup of coffee and a place to let your guard down. For her, that space is ***StephanieMayWilson.com***, where she shares stories of big adventures and small moments with friends and strangers alike.

Follow her on Instagram and Twitter @smaywilson.

Made in the USA
Columbia, SC
13 October 2018